**JESSIE KANELOS WEINER**

PHOTOGRAPHS BY RICHARD BOUTIN

# PUNCHES

## *& Infused Rums*

weldon**owen**

# Contents

## PUNCHES

## INFUSED RUMS

## FINGER FOOD

# PUNCH
## *Classic*
### agreeably fruity

**Makes 3½ quarts**
**Prep 10 minutes**
**Chilling 2 hours**

1 qt (32 fl oz) fruit juice
    blend
1 qt (32 fl oz) orange juice
3⅓ cups white rum
¾ cup cane syrup
2 oranges
2 apples
Ice cubes

In a serving bowl, combine the fruit juice blend, orange juice, rum, and cane syrup.

Cut the oranges and apples into slices, then cut the orange slices into pieces. Add them to the rum mixture. Stir well and chill for at least 2 hours.

Just before serving, add ice cubes.

## PUNCH
# *Lemon*
### very refreshing

**Makes 3½ quarts**
**Prep 10 minutes**
**Chilling 2 hours**

1 cup granulated sugar

2 cups lemon juice
    (about 10 lemons)

2 cups vodka, well chilled

3 bottles Champagne
    or other sparkling wine

2 whole lemons, thinly
    sliced and cut into pieces

In a serving bowl, dissolve the sugar in the lemon juice. Pour in the vodka and stir. Chill for at least 2 hours.

Just before serving, add the Champagne and the lemon slices. Mix well.

# Pink Lemonade

like a summer breeze

**Makes 3½ quarts**
**Prep 10 minutes**
**Chilling 2 hours**

2 cups lemon juice
  (about 10 lemons)
2 cups strawberry juice
1 cup cane syrup
1 qt water
1 cup vodka
3⅓ cups strawberries
2 whole lemons
1⅔ cups raspberries

In a serving bowl, combine the lemon juice, strawberry juice, cane syrup, water, and vodka. Chill for at least 2 hours.

Hull the strawberries and, depending on their size, halve or quarter them. Cut the lemons into small pieces.

Add the strawberries, raspberries, and lemon pieces to the vodka mixture. Mix well and serve at once.

**PUNCH**

# Ginger

spicy & invigorating

**Makes 3½ quarts**
**Prep 35 minutes**
**Chilling 2 hours**

3 cups ginger syrup, store-bought or homemade*

3 cups gin, well chilled

3 cups lime juice (about 24 limes)

3 limes

3-inch knob fresh ginger (about 1½ oz)

6 cups (48 fl oz) sparkling water, well chilled

Ice cubes

*Homemade ginger syrup:

2 cups granulated sugar

2 cups water

1⅓ cups peeled and chopped fresh ginger (about 7 oz)

To make ginger syrup, in a medium saucepan, dissolve the sugar in the water over medium heat. Add the peeled and chopped ginger and simmer for 15 minutes. Let cool, then strain the syrup through a fine-mesh sieve.

In a serving bowl, combine the gin, lime juice, and ginger syrup. Chill for at least 2 hours.

Thinly slice the limes and ginger. Add the sparkling water, lime slices, ginger slices, and ice cubes to the gin mixture. Stir well and serve at once.

# PUNCH
## *Apple*
### a taste of autumn

**Makes 3½ quarts**
**Prep 10 minutes**
**Chilling 2 hours**

6 cups apple cider or juice,
   well chilled

4 cinnamon sticks

2 vanilla pods

1⅔ cups whiskey, chilled

1 liter (33.8 fl oz) ginger ale,
   chilled

Juice of 5 lemons

3 apples (3 different
   varieties, ideally)

Pour the apple cider into a serving bowl. Add the cinnamon sticks. Halve the vanilla pods lengthwise and scrape out the seeds with the point of a knife into the cider, then add the pods. Chill for at least 2 hours.

Add the whiskey, ginger ale, and lemon juice to the cider mixture. Stir well. Core and slice the apples, add to the punch, and serve at once.

# Springtime
fresh as the month of May

**Makes 3½ quarts**
**Prep 35 minutes**

4 cups (32 fl oz) rhubarb
    syrup, store-bought or
    homemade*

1 bunch fresh mint

2 green apples

4 cups (32 fl oz) apple cider
    or apple juice, well chilled

2 cups vodka, well chilled

1 liter (33.8 fl oz) sparkling
    water

Ice cubes


*Homemade rhubarb syrup:

8 large stalks rhubarb,
    trimmed and chopped

2½ cups granulated sugar

2 cups water

To make rhubarb syrup, combine the rhubarb, sugar, and water in a saucepan. Place over medium heat and simmer until the rhubarb is very tender, 20 minutes. Strain through a fine-mesh sieve, pressing the rhubarb with the back of a spoon to extract as much flavor as possible. Let the syrup cool completely.

Pluck the mint leaves and cut the apples into thin slices. In a serving bowl, combine the rhubarb syrup, cider, vodka, mint leaves, and apple slices.

Just before serving, add the sparkling water and ice cubes. Mix well.

## PUNCH
# Copacabana
### a round-trip to sunny shores

**Makes 3 quarts**
**Prep 10 minutes**
**Chilling 2 hours**

3 cups pineapple juice,
   well chilled

3 cups orange juice,
   well chilled

2½ cups coconut water,
   well chilled

2 cups white rum with
   coconut liqueur (such
   as Malibu brand)

¾ cup triple sec

¾ cup lime juice
   (about 6 limes)

3 kiwis

2 whole limes

1 small Victoria pineapple

2 passion fruits

Ice cubes

In a serving bowl, combine the pineapple juice, orange juice, coconut water, rum with coconut liqueur, triple sec, and lime juice. Chill for at least 2 hours.

Peel and slice the kiwis and limes, then peel, core, and cut the pineapple into pieces. Halve the passion fruits and scoop out the pulp. Add the sliced fruits, passion fruit pulp, and ice cubes to the rum mixture. Serve at once.

# Cherry Blossom

## delicate as a flower in bloom

**Makes 3 quarts**
**Prep 10 minutes**
**Chilling 2 hours**

5 cups lychee juice,
  well chilled*

2 cups apple juice,
  well chilled

2 cups sake, well chilled

2 cups vodka, well chilled

Juice of 2 lemons

1 whole green apple

1 cup canned pitted lychees,
  drained

Ice cubes

*Available in Asian markets

In a serving bowl, combine the lychee juice, apple juice, sake, vodka, and lemon juice. Chill for at least 2 hours.

Thinly slice the apple, then cut out flowers using a flower-shaped cookie cutter or a fluted canelé mold ¾ inch in diameter.

Just before serving, add the apple flowers, lychees, and ice cubes to the vodka mixture.

## PUNCH Sunrise

a new day dawns

**Makes 3½ quarts**
**Prep 15 minutes**
**Freezing 6 hours**

2 pomegranates, seeded
Ice cubes
5 cups orange juice
5 cups cranberry juice
1⅔ cups tequila
2 oranges

Put the pomegranate seeds in the bottom of a ring mold. Cover with ice cubes to keep the seeds at the bottom of the mold, then fill with water. Place in the freezer for at least 6 hours.

In a serving bowl, combine the orange juice, cranberry juice, and tequila. Slice the oranges, cut them into pieces, then add to the tequila mixture. Chill for at least 2 hours.

Pour a little hot water onto the ring mold to release the ring of ice, then place it in the serving bowl with the tequila mixture. Serve.

PUNCH

# Ruby Red

a study in scarlet

**Makes 2½ quarts**
**Prep 20 minutes**
**Chilling 2 hours**

3 tablespoons rooibos tea
   or black tea

1⅔ cups boiling water

2 cups Aperol (bitter
   orange aperitif)

2 cups white rum

2 cups blood orange juice

1⅔ cups pomegranate juice

4 whole blood oranges

1 whole pomegranate,
   seeded

Ice cubes

Steep the tea in the boiling water. Let cool and strain through a fine-mesh sieve.

In a serving bowl, combine the tea, Aperol, rum, blood orange juice, and pomegranate juice. Chill for at least 2 hours.

Cut the blood oranges into slices and add them, along with the pomegranate seeds and ice cubes, to the rum mixture. Serve at once.

# PUNCH Tropical

### perfumed with island fruits

**Makes 3½ quarts**
**Prep 15 minutes**
**Chilling 2 hours**

2½ cups mango nectar

2½ cups pineapple juice

2½ cups orange juice

2½ cups dark rum

1¼ cups Cointreau or
   other triple sec

1¼ cups lime juice
   (about 10 limes)

2 vanilla pods

3 whole limes, sliced

3 whole mandarin oranges,
   sliced

1 small Victoria pineapple,
   peeled, cored, and cut
   into pieces

In a serving bowl, combine the mango nectar, pineapple juice, orange juice, rum, Cointreau, and lime juice. Halve the vanilla pods lengthwise and scrape out the seeds with the point of a knife into the bowl, then add the pods. Chill for at least 2 hours.

Remove the vanilla pods from the rum mixture and add the sliced and cut-up fruits. Stir well and serve at once.

## PUNCH
# Citrus
### agreeably · sparkling

**Makes 3½ quarts**
**Prep 10 minutes**
**Chilling 1 hour**

2½ cups orange juice

2½ cups grapefruit juice

2 cups lemon juice

1⅔ cups cane syrup

1¼ cups triple sec

1 whole grapefruit, sliced

2 lemons, sliced

2 limes, sliced

4 oz kumquats, sliced

1 bottle Champagne or
   other sparkling wine

Ice cubes

In a serving bowl, combine the orange juice, grapefruit juice, lemon juice, cane syrup, and triple sec. Chill for at least 1 hour.

Add the sliced citrus, then pour in the Champagne. Add ice cubes and serve at once.

# PUNCH
## *Elderberry*
### sweetly garnished with elderflowers

**Makes 3½ quarts**
**Prep 10 minutes**
**Chilling 2 hours**

⅔ cup granulated sugar

1 cup lemon juice

2 cups cranberry juice,
 well chilled

1⅔ cups elderberry liqueur
 (such as Saint-Germain
 brand)

2 lemons, thinly sliced

3 bottles Champagne or
 other sparkling wine

Fresh elderflowers for
 garnish (optional)

In a serving bowl, dissolve the sugar in the lemon juice.
Add the cranberry juice and elderberry liqueur, then stir.
Chill for at least 2 hours.

Add the sliced lemons and Champagne. Decorate the
bowl with elderflowers, if desired, and serve.

# Clementine

## full of pep

**Makes 3½ quarts**
**Prep 10 minutes**
**Chilling 2 hours**

2 qts clementine juice
3¼ cups orange juice
2 cups tequila
1 bunch fresh mint
3 whole clementines
3 limes

In a serving bowl, combine the clementine juice, orange juice, and tequila. Chill for at least 2 hours.

Pluck the mint leaves and cut the clementines and limes into slices. Add the mint leaves and the sliced fruits to the tequila mixture. Mix well and serve.

# PUNCH
# Christmas Eve
## while waiting for Santa...

**Makes 3½ quarts**
**Prep 15 minutes**
**Chilling 2 hours**

1⅔ cups orange juice

1⅔ cups cranberry juice

1⅔ cups pineapple juice

3 tablespoons Cognac

¾ cup Grand Marnier or
other triple sec

¾ cup white rum

4 cinnamon sticks

4 pods star anise

2 vanilla pods

3 whole clementines

12 whole cloves

1 Victoria pineapple

2 bottles Champagne or
other sparkling wine

In a serving bowl, combine the orange juice, cranberry juice, pineapple juice, Cognac, Grand Marnier, rum, cinnamon sticks, and star anise. Halve the vanilla pods lengthwise and scrape out the seeds with the point of a knife into the bowl, then add the pods. Stir. Chill for at least 2 hours.

Thinly slice the clementines and stud them with the whole cloves. Peel, core, and cut the pineapple into pieces. Add the fruits to the Cognac mixture and pour in the Champagne. Serve at once.

**PUNCH**

# Bloody Mary

the brunchtime essential

**Makes 3½ quarts**
**Prep 5 minutes**
**Chilling 2 hours**

5 cups tomato juice

1⅔ cups vodka

2 tablespoons
Worcestershire sauce

1 teaspoon celery salt

¼ teaspoon cayenne

Juice of 4 lemons

4–5 whole lemons

2 limes

1 cucumber for garnish

Pimiento-stuffed green
olives
for garnish

1 head celery

Tabasco sauce

Salt and pepper

In a serving pitcher, combine the tomato juice, vodka, Worcestershire sauce, celery salt, cayenne, and lemon juice. Taste and adjust the seasoning if necessary. Slice 1 of the lemons and the limes. Add to the vodka mixture and mix well. Chill for at least 2 hours.

Cut the remaining lemons into slices. Slice the cucumber crosswise and cut each slice into quarters. Thread cucumber quarters and olives onto cocktail picks. Garnish each serving glass with a lemon slice, a cucumber-olive pick, a celery rib, and a dash of Tabasco.

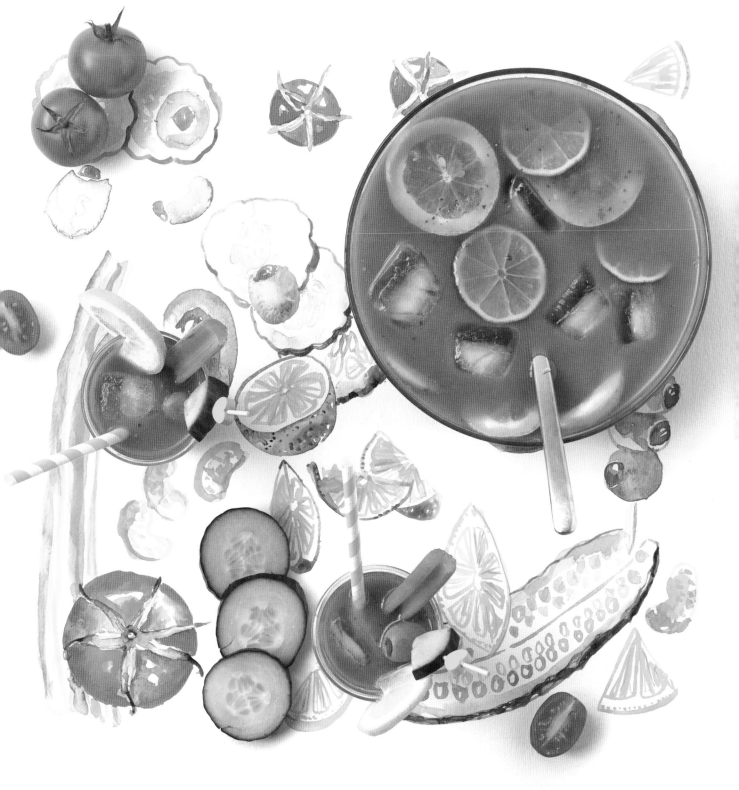

# PUNCH

## Cucumber

with fresh flavors of lime & basil

**Makes 3½ quarts**
**Prep 5 minutes**
**Chilling 2 hours**

2 cups cucumber juice*
2 cups gin
2 cups lime juice
    (about 16 limes)
1 small cucumber
1 bunch basil
2 whole limes, sliced
6¼ cups (50 fl oz) tonic
    water
Ice cubes

*Homemade cucumber juice:
    1 medium cucumber

To make cucumber juice, peel and dice the medium cucumber. Place in a food processor and add enough water to just cover the cucumber. Blend to a smooth liquid. Strain through a sieve and set aside.

In a serving bowl, combine the cucumber juice, gin, and lime juice. Slice the small cucumber crosswise and cut each slice into quarters. Pluck a few attractive leaves from the basil bunch and reserve for garnishing. Add the cucumber quarters, remaining basil bunch, and lime slices to the gin mixture. Chill for at least 2 hours.

Just before serving, remove the basil bunch from the punch. Pour in the tonic water, add ice cubes, and garnish with the reserved basil leaves.

## PUNCH
# Coconut
### so smooth

**Makes 3 quarts**
**Prep 10 minutes**
**Chilling 12 hours**

1½ cups fresh coconut meat
    (divided)

6 limes (divided)

Ice cubes

2 cups white rum

2 cups cane syrup

2 cups lime juice
    (about 16 limes)

2 cups coconut water

2 cups coconut milk

Cut half of the coconut meat into small pieces, as well as 3 of the limes. Place the fruit in the bottom of a ring mold. Cover with ice cubes to keep the fruit at the bottom of the mold, then fill with water. Place in the freezer for about 12 hours.

In a serving bowl, combine the rum, cane syrup, lime juice, and coconut water and milk. Cut up and add the remaining coconut meat and limes. Chill for at least 2 hours.

Pour a little hot water onto the ring mold to release the ring of ice, then place it in the serving bowl with the rum mixture. Serve at once.

# INFUSED RUM

## *Lime*

### the vanilla-scented classic

**Makes 1 quart**
**Prep 5 minutes**
**Infusing 3 weeks**

2 vanilla pods
Zest of 2 limes
3¼ cups white rum
⅓ cup lime juice
   (about 3 limes)
⅔ cup cane syrup

Halve the vanilla pods lengthwise and scrape out the seeds with the point of a knife into a jar or bottle. Add the pods to the jar, along with the lime zest. Combine the rum, lime juice, and cane syrup, then pour this mixture into the jar or bottle.

Close the jar or bottle with an airtight lid or cap and let infuse at room temperature for at least 3 weeks before serving.

# Piña Colada

## a tropical concoction

**Makes 1 quart**
**Prep 5 minutes**
**Infusing 3 weeks**

¾ cup fresh coconut meat

⅔ cup pineapple chunks

⅓ cup cane syrup

2½ cups white rum

⅓ cup white rum with coconut liqueur (such as Malibu brand)

Dice the coconut meat and pineapple.

Combine the cane syrup, rum, and rum with coconut liqueur, then pour into a jar or bottle. Add the diced fruit.

Close the jar or bottle with an airtight lid or cap and let infuse at room temperature for at least 3 weeks before serving.

## INFUSED RUM
# Gingerbread
### warm & spicy

**Makes 1 quart**
**Prep 5 minutes**
**Infusing 3 weeks**

½ cup honey

1¼ cups dark rum

2½ cups white rum

2 cinnamon sticks

1¼-inch knob fresh ginger, peeled and sliced

Zest of 2 oranges

1 pod star anise

2 whole cloves

½ whole nutmeg

Combine the honey and rums and stir until the honey is incorporated.

Put the cinnamon sticks, sliced ginger, orange zest, star anise, cloves, and nutmeg in a jar or bottle. Pour in the rum-honey mixture. Mix well, then close the jar or bottle with an airtight lid or cap.

Let infuse at room temperature for at least 3 weeks before serving.

# Peach & Ginger
### soft as peach fuzz

**Makes 1 quart**
**Prep 5 minutes**
**Infusing 3 weeks**

3 ripe peaches
1½-inch knob fresh ginger
   (about ¾ oz)
¼ cup honey
3⅓ cups white rum

Pit and slice the peaches, then slice the ginger. Put the peaches and ginger in a jar or bottle.

Combine the honey and rum and stir until the honey is incorporated. Pour into the jar or bottle to cover the peaches and ginger.

Close the jar or bottle with an airtight lid or cap and let infuse at room temperature for at least 3 weeks before serving.

## INFUSED RUM

# Passion

### intense & perfumed

**Makes 1 quart**
**Prep 5 minutes**
**Infusing 3 weeks**

2 vanilla pods
5 passion fruits
Zest of 2 limes
⅓ cup cane syrup
3⅓ cups white rum

Halve the vanilla pods lengthwise and scrape out the seeds with the point of a knife into a jar or bottle. Add the pods to the jar. Scoop the passion fruit pulp into the jar or bottle, and add the lime zest.

Combine the cane syrup and the rum, then pour into the jar or bottle. Close the jar or bottle with an airtight lid or cap and let infuse at room temperature for at least 3 weeks before serving.

## INFUSED RUM
# Mixed Berry
### woodland fruits

**Makes 1 quart**
**Prep 5 minutes**
**Infusing 3 weeks**

1 vanilla pod

⅓–½ cup strawberries, hulled and halved

½ cup raspberries

¼ cup blueberries

¼ cup red currants, if available, or additional blueberries

⅓ cup cane syrup

3⅓ cups white rum

Halve the vanilla pod lengthwise and scrape out the seeds with the point of a knife into a jar or bottle. Add the pod to the jar, along with the berries.

Combine the cane syrup and the rum, then pour into the jar or bottle. Close the jar or bottle with an airtight lid or cap and let infuse at room temperature for at least 3 weeks before serving.

## INFUSED RUM
# Three Grapes
### the aroma of harvest time

**Makes 1 quart**
**Prep 5 minutes**
**Infusing 3 weeks**

⅔ cup green grapes
⅔ cup red grapes
⅔ cup black grapes
⅓ cup cane syrup
6 cups white rum

Halve the grapes lengthwise, then put them in a jar or bottle.

Combine the cane syrup and the rum, then pour into the jar or bottle. Close the jar or bottle with an airtight lid or cap and let infuse at room temperature for at least 3 weeks before serving.

# INFUSED RUM
## *Coffee*
### with vanilla & maple syrup

**Makes 1 quart**
**Prep 5 minutes**
**Infusing 3 weeks**

2 vanilla pods
½ cup coffee beans
⅔ cup maple syrup
3⅓ cups dark rum

Halve the vanilla pods lengthwise and scrape out the seeds with the point of a knife into a jar or bottle. Add the pods to the jar, along with the coffee beans.

Combine the maple syrup and the rum, then pour into the jar or bottle. Close the jar or bottle with an airtight lid or cap and let infuse at room temperature for at least 3 weeks before serving.

# INFUSED RUM
## *Tropical*
### bright & sunny

**Makes 1 quart**
**Prep 5 minutes**
**Infusing 3 weeks**

⅓ cup pineapple chunks
　(2 oz)
⅓ cup mango chunks (2 oz)
3 kumquats
1 vanilla pod
2 passion fruits
⅓ cup cane syrup
3⅓ cups white rum

Dice the pineapple and mango, and slice the kumquats. Halve the vanilla pod lengthwise and scrape out the seeds with the point of a knife into a jar or bottle. Add the pod to the jar, along with the diced and sliced fruits. Scoop the passion fruit pulp into the jar, and pour in the cane syrup and rum. Mix well.

Close the jar or bottle with an airtight lid or cap and let infuse at room temperature for at least 3 weeks before serving.

# PIÑA COLADA *Shrimp*
### salty & sweet

**Makes 20 shrimp**
**Prep 15 minutes**
**Cooking 8–10 minutes**

### PINEAPPLE SAUCE
⅔ cup pineapple chunks
   (4 oz)

Juice of 1 lime

1 teaspoon honey

1 teaspoon minced
   red onion

½ teaspoon minced
   red chile

1 teaspoon chopped cilantro

Pinch salt

### SHRIMP
8 oz raw large shrimp
   (about 20), peeled with
   tail segments left intact

Salt and pepper

2 egg whites

½ cup grated dried coconut

1 cup dried bread crumbs

1 tablespoon cornstarch

Pinch cayenne

2 tablespoons olive oil

To make the pineapple sauce, dice the pineapple and combine with the lime juice and honey in a food processor. Blend to a smooth purée. Blend in the red onion and chile, then the cilantro and salt. Set aside.

Preheat the oven to 450°F. Season the shrimp with salt and pepper. Whisk the egg whites until foamy. In a shallow bowl, mix the coconut, bread crumbs, cornstarch, 2 pinches of salt, and the cayenne. Dip the shrimp in the egg whites. Shake gently to remove the excess, then roll them in the coconut–bread crumb mixture to bread them.

Divide the shrimp between two parchment paper–lined baking sheets. Brush them with the olive oil, then bake until the coconut breading is golden brown and the shrimp are pink. Serve with the pineapple sauce.

# BLOODY MARY
## *Gazpacho*
### an eye-catching appetizer

**Makes about 15 shots**
**Prep 20 minutes**

3 cucumbers

1 small tomato

2 green onions

½ small red bell pepper

1 tablespoon red wine
vinegar

Juice of ½ lime

4 tablespoons olive oil

1 teaspoon Worcestershire
sauce

½ teaspoon celery salt

Espelette pepper or good-
quality hot paprika

1 head celery

Pimiento-stuffed green
olives for garnish

Salt and pepper

Cut the cucumbers into 1½-inch lengths. Using a melon baller, dig out hollows about 1¼ inches deep, without piercing all the way through, to make little shot glasses. Reserve the cucumber flesh.

Dice the tomato, mince the green onions, and seed and cut the bell pepper into pieces. In a food processor, combine ½ cup cucumber flesh, the tomato, green onions, bell pepper, vinegar, lime juice, olive oil, Worcestershire sauce, celery salt, and a pinch of Espelette pepper. Blend to a smooth and even consistency, still keeping some texture. Taste and adjust the seasoning.

Pour the mixture into the cucumber shot glasses. Sprinkle each with a pinch of Espelette pepper and garnish with a rib of celery and a green olive threaded onto a cocktail pick. Serve at once.

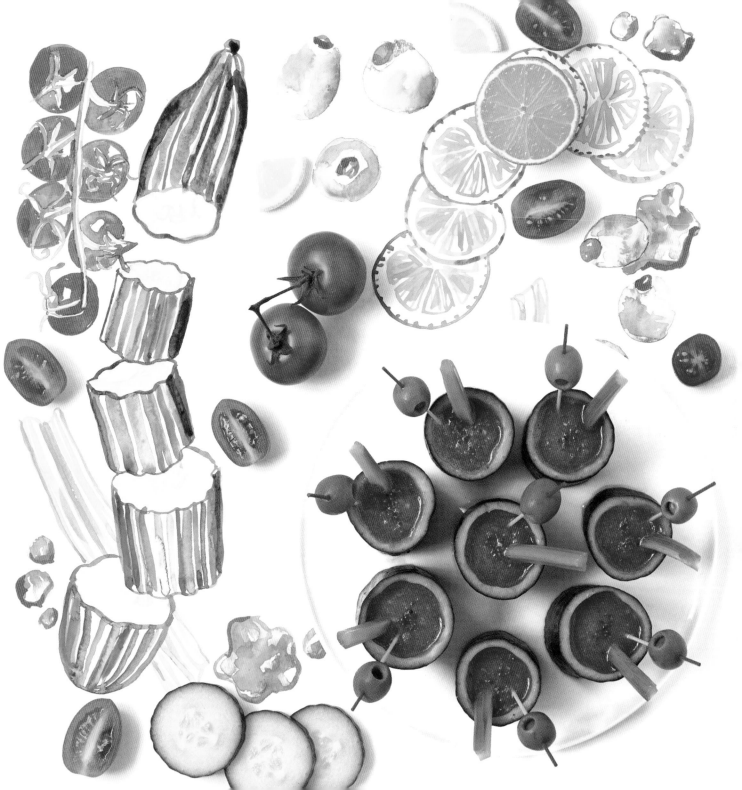

# MARGARITA
## *Ceviche*
### an ocean of freshness

**Makes 10 little glassfuls**
**Prep 15 minutes**
**Chilling 10 minutes**

7 oz cod

⅔ cup lime juice

1 clove garlic, minced

¾-inch knob fresh ginger, peeled and minced

4 cilantro sprigs

2 oranges

1 green onion

2½ tablespoons sea salt, preferably fleur de sel

½ teaspoon Espelette pepper or good-quality hot paprika

1 lime, cut into rounds and rounds halved

Cut the fish into ¼-inch dice. In a serving bowl, combine the lime juice, garlic, and ginger. Pluck the cilantro leaves from the stems. Chop the stems and add them to the marinade. Reserve the cilantro leaves. Let the fish marinate for 5 minutes.

Strain the marinade through a fine-mesh sieve, then completely cover the fish in the marinade again. Chill for 10 minutes.

Supreme the oranges by peeling them with a sharp knife and cutting between each membrane to free the segments. Mince the green onion. Add the orange supremes and green onion to the marinating fish, and mix.

In a shallow bowl, combine the salt and Espelette pepper. Rub the rims of 10 glasses with a lime slice, then dip the moistened rims into the salt mixture.

Divide the marinated fish among the glasses. Chop the cilantro leaves and sprinkle over the ceviche. Decorate each with a half-round of lime. Serve at once.

# COSMOPOLITAN
# Chicken Brochettes
charming finger food

**Makes 10–15 cocktail skewers**
**Prep 20 minutes**
**Chilling 2 hours**
**Cooking 5 minutes**

### MARINATED CHICKEN
3–4 tablespoons cranberry juice

Juice of 1 lime

¾-inch knob fresh ginger, peeled and minced

1 clove garlic, peeled and crushed

10 oz boneless, skinless chicken breast, cut into ¾-inch pieces

### COSMOPOLITAN SAUCE
½ cup ketchup or tomato sauce

¼ cup honey

Juice of 2 limes

Juice of 1 orange

1 tablespoon soy sauce

10–15 bamboo cocktail skewers

Salt and pepper

2 green onions, thinly sliced

1 small handful cilantro, leaves chopped

1 teaspoon sesame seeds

To make the marinade, in a large bowl, stir together the cranberry juice, lime juice, ginger, and garlic. Add the chicken pieces, stir to coat, cover, and let marinate in the refrigerator for at least 2 hours.

To prepare the Cosmopolitan sauce, in a saucepan, combine the ketchup, honey, lime juice, orange juice, and soy sauce. Place over medium heat and bring to a simmer. Let simmer for 5 minutes.

Preheat the broiler. Soak the skewers in water to prevent scorching during cooking.

Drain the chicken pieces and thread them onto the skewers (about 4 per skewer). Place them on a parchment paper–lined baking sheet. Season, then broil for 2 minutes. Turn the skewers and broil for 2 minutes more.

With a brush, coat the chicken skewers with the Cosmopolitan sauce and broil until caramelized, 1 minute longer. Upon removing them from the oven, coat the skewers again with sauce. Sprinkle with sliced green onion, a little chopped cilantro, and sesame seeds. Serve at once.

# MARTINI
# *Olive Straws*

## 007's favorite

**Makes about 16 straws**
**Prep 15 minutes**
**Freezing 1 hour**
**Cooking 5-6 minutes**

1 sheet pure butter
    puff pastry

1 egg, beaten

Zest of 1 lemon

16 pimiento-stuffed
    large green olives

Using a rolling pin, roll out the puff pastry sheet into a rectangle of about 12 inches by 6 inches. Cut into two smaller rectangles, making one rectangle of 5 inches by 6 inches, then a second one of 7 inches by 6 inches.

Brush the smaller rectangle with the beaten egg and sprinkle it with the lemon zest. With a long edge of the dough facing you, arrange the olives in 4 rows of 4 olives each, end to end but with a small space in between each olive, from the top to the bottom edges. Cover with the larger rectangle of pastry. Press down the pastry firmly between each olive, and pinch the edges together to seal them. Freeze for 1 hour.

Preheat the oven to 450°F. With a short edge of the dough facing you, cut the pastry rectangle into 4 strips, cutting between each row of olives. Then, slicing through the olives, cut each strip into 4 straws (each olive is cut into 4 slices). You should have 16 straws.

Place the straws flat side down on a parchment paper–lined baking sheet and bake until the pastry is golden brown, 5-6 minutes. Serve.

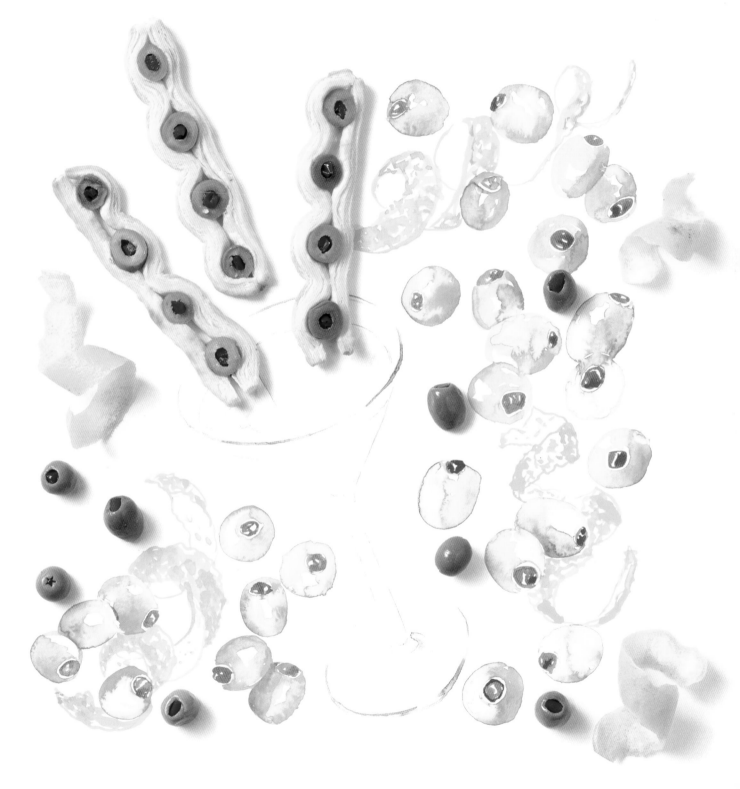

# weldon**owen**

Published in North America by Weldon Owen, Inc.
1045 Sansome Street, Suite 100, San Francisco, CA 94111
www.weldonowen.com
Weldon Owen is a division of Bonnier Publishing USA

Originally published in 2015 as *Punchs & Rhums Arrangés*

© Hachette Livre (Marabout) 2016

Illustrations by Jessie Kanelos Weiner
Photographs by Richard Boutin
English translation by Sarah Putman Clegg

Library of Congress Cataloging-in-Publication data is available

ISBN 13: 978-1-68188-192-8
ISBN 10: 1-68188-192-6

Printed in China

This edition printed in 2016
10  9  8  7  6  5  4  3  2  1